Putting On an Act

by Paul Mason
illustrated by Carlos Aon

Chapter 1

At Camp

The scout leader finished assigning the different dens to tents and then told the scouts to get settled in. The boys grabbed their backpacks and ran down to the campsite.

Carlos and his friend Logan quickly found the Tiger den's tent. "Mine," Carlos said, flinging himself onto one of the cots.

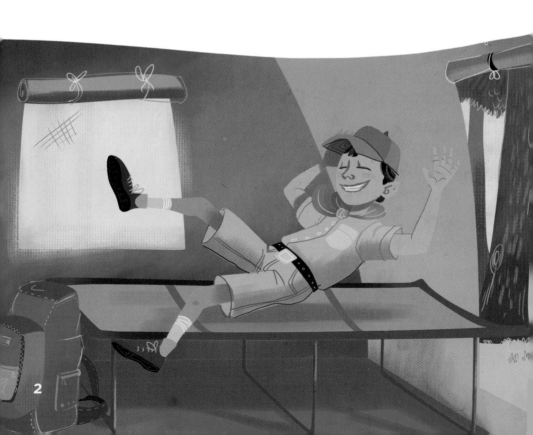

Logan stared out at the forest that surrounded the field like a wall of trees. "I hope there are plenty of insects out there. I need to find a few more species for my insect study badge."

"Nature is nice to look at," said Carlos, "but if you can't throw it, dribble it, or score points with it, I'm not interested."

Logan chuckled. "Well, we're hiking the nature trail this afternoon. You might change your mind."

Carlos shrugged and put his things away. "I can't wait to get onto the archery range," he said.

STOP AND CHECK

How does Logan feel about being in the forest?

Chapter 2

On Target

Carlos drew another arrow from his quiver. He clicked the groove at the end of it into place on the string. He raised the bow, pulled back on the string, and took aim at the target across the field.

His arms trembled as he let the arrow fly, but it shot through the air like a thunderbolt and thudded into the target. The arrow hit close to the middle of the yellow ring.

"Not bad," Carlos thought. He almost had the points he needed to beat his best score. He was sure the last arrow would do it.

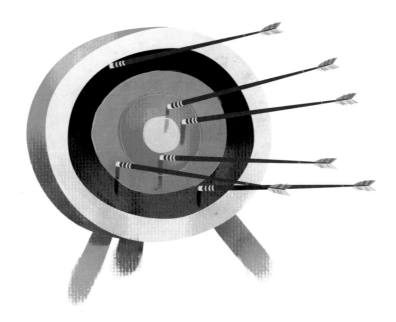

Carlos pulled the string back and took aim once more.

"Okay, finish up the quiver you're on," the archery instructor called. "Then we'll break for lunch."

Carlos let loose. Again the arrow shot into the target with a thud. Carlos peered at the place where his arrow hit. This time it was buried in the black ring near the edge. That wasn't so good.

Carlos frowned. He'd been distracted by the instructor. Just when he was getting into his groove, they were taking a break. And after that, they would be off on a nature hike.

"Why can't we just do sports all day?" Carlos said to Logan. "Why do we have to go on a hike?" he grumbled.

"Come on, Carlos, it'll be fun," Logan said. "We might see a bear!"

Carlos still felt grumpy.

STOP AND CHECK

Why doesn't Carlos want to go on the nature hike?

Chapter 3 A Cry in the Valley

After lunch, the Tigers set off on their hike. The other boys charged into the forest, but Carlos dragged his feet, dropping back to the end of the line. He could see Logan and the den leader chatting at the front.

They followed the trail until it left the woods and sloped down through a valley covered in grass and scrub. Carlos slowly shuffled through the brittle twigs, letting the others get even farther ahead.

Then Carlos heard something that made him stop. It was a high-pitched cry, as shrill as a whistle. It sounded like someone in pain. The valley was silent for a moment, but then he heard the call again.

Carlos stared at the grass along the path. At first he couldn't spot what was making the sound. Then he saw something move.

A small brown bird was flapping around on the ground just off the trail. It was twittering loudly. Carlos could see that one of its wings was outstretched. "It looks like its wing is broken," he thought.

Carlos stood still and watched the bird, fascinated. It was a splotchy brown color, with a white chest and a pattern of black rings around its neck.

Carlos followed the bird as it dragged itself along the ground. "Hey, bird. What's up with you?" he said quietly. If he could catch it and take it back to camp, maybe they could fix its wing.

STOP AND CHECK

What happened when Carlos fell behind on the nature walk?

Chapter 4

The Killdeer

Footsteps and shouting announced the return of the other Tigers, who had come back to find Carlos.

"Rule number one, Carlos," said the den leader sternly. "Always stay with the den." Then he saw what Carlos was pointing at. "Ah," he said, "looks like you found a killdeer."

"That little thing kills deer?" asked Carlos, stepping back from the bird.

The den leader smiled, "No. The name 'killdeer' is descriptive. It's what the bird's call usually sounds like. But right now it's doing something quite different."

The scouts gathered around to watch the bird. The killdeer called out again and began spinning around in circles like a top. It was fluttering both wings now.

"It's hurt," said Carlos.

"There's nothing wrong with it," said the den leader. "It just wants you to think there is."

"Why would it do that?" asked Carlos, surprised.

"You're the scout, you figure it out," the leader challenged him. "Come on, Tigers, let's go. No falling behind this time, Carlos."

Carlos took a last look at the little bird. He never knew birds could pretend. Perhaps there was more to nature than he'd thought.

Back at camp, Carlos found a book on local wildlife and began flipping though it.

"I thought you weren't interested in nature," said Logan.

"Yeah, well, this bird is interesting. Check this out," Carlos said, reading aloud.

"'The killdeer is famous for its broken wing distraction. It does this to lead predators away from its young.' That's what it was doing."

"So a bird fooled you into following it?"

"I guess," said Carlos. "I must have gotten too close to its nest, and so it started acting like easy prey to draw me away from its babies. Wow, that's creative!" Carlos pulled out his logbook and started making notes.

"You're writing about nature? Now I've seen everything," Logan teased.

Carlos laughed. "Making up for lost time," he said. "I've decided to go for the bird study badge!"

STOP AND CHECK

Why does Carlos change his mind about nature?

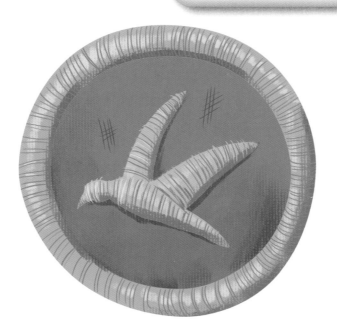

Respond to Reading

Summarize

Use details from *Putting On an Act* to summarize the story. Your graphic organizer may help.

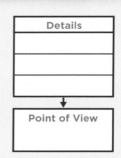

Details

↓

Point of View

Text Evidence

1. How do you know that *Putting On an Act* is realistic fiction? **GENRE**

2. Who tells this story? Use details from the text to explain how you know. **POINT OF VIEW**

3. What does the author compare to a "thunderbolt" on page 4? What does the phrase "like a thunderbolt" mean? **FIGURATIVE LANGUAGE**

4. Write a description of the nature hike that Carlos could have written. Use pronouns such as *I*, *me*, and *my* to show what Carlos thinks and feels. **WRITE ABOUT READING**

Compare Text
Read some haiku that have been inspired by animals.

Broken Wing

Broken wing flailing

Beckons the cat to follow.

Chicks hide behind grass.

Rat

Sunset painted field

Footfall brushes against wheat

Sending rat scuttling.

Seal

Silent ribbon drifts.

Idle seal floats on the tide,

Relishing thick eel.

Make Connections

How did animals inspire the writers of these haiku?
ESSENTIAL QUESTION

Why does the killdeer inspire the writers of *Putting On an Act* and *Broken Wing*? TEXT TO TEXT

Focus on Genre

Poetry Poetry often uses figurative language such as simile and metaphor to describe something. Haiku are short poems that have 17 syllables in three lines of 5, 7, and 5.

Read and Find Each haiku in the paired selection is inspired by an animal. In "Seal," the writer uses a metaphor to describe the eel that the seal eats. Reread this haiku. Find the metaphor. How does it help describe the animal?

Your Turn

With a partner, choose a photograph or illustration of an animal that interests you. Use this as your inspiration to write a haiku. Remember to use language features such as simile and metaphor to describe the animal.

To write a haiku, start by writing longer lines, then cut each line back until you find the best way to describe the animal with the correct number of syllables.

Display the haiku you wrote next to the image you used for inspiration.